THE
Archive Photographs
SERIES

WOODHOUSE

Woodhouse village cricket team c. 1910. The man with moustache (seated, front) is William Widdowson.

The bad winter of 1947 caused many accidents and Woodhouse Mill was no exception – here a bus has left the road and 'dived' into the Rother.

An old 'tinglelary' or portable organ is part of a fund raising 'Self Denial' for the Salvation Army in 1907. This picture was probably taken outside their old headquarters on Tannery Street.

The old chapel in the cemetery on Revill Lane. This chapel served the needs of all religious denominations during burials but was demolished many years ago.

The Quaker chapel on Meetinghouse Lane *c.* 1900. The Society of Friends or Quakers were formed in 1668 by George Fox to engage in missionary work. The Society emphasises a plainess of dress and a refusal to take part in activities regarded as 'frivolous'. Before the Toleration Act of 1689 Quakers were persecuted for their beliefs; a hang over of this persecution would lead to men and women sitting on opposing sides during their meetings. If a raid occurred the women and children could leave as group unmolested by the authorities. The Society rejects the sacraments and most set forms of worship and have a strong commitment to pacifism. Today this 'chapel' or 'meetinghouse' is a private home.

Two
At the Heart
of Woodhouse

A picture of the Market Place at the turn of the century. In the background is situated C.E. Rollinson's Boot factory with the tempting advertisement 'Try our 3s 11d pit boots'. Next door to the boot emporium was the York City and County Banking Corporation which was only open on Mondays, Wednesdays and Fridays. In 1909 the Corporation was bought by the London Joint Stock Bank which became part of the Midland Bank in 1918. 'Market Place' was later changed to Market Square but for this section and for ease of reference I have used the former name.

The Market Place *c.* 1900 with Rollinson's boot factory in the background.

The same buildings on the corner of the Market Place just before demolition *c.* 1965. The shop are the grocery store and beer off on the left; Lax's fish and chip shop, the snack bar, Peggy Hairdressing, W. Dickinson's.

A view from the Market Place looking down Market Street *c.* 1890. The Woodhouse Cross was rected in 1775 by Joshua Littlewood on the site of an earlier monument. In 1826 a sun dial and veather vane were added; the pillar was replaced in 1897 along with the crumbling top step. adly, the vane and dial were stolen after the war but have (at the time of writing) just been eplaced.

A similar view down Market Street taken in the 1960s just before many of these buildings were emolished. Pictured here is Mrs Smith's sweet shop and to the extreme left is Fox's Drapery nop which had been in the Woodhouse cinema building. The first cinema in Woodhouse was ased at the Central Hall on Church Lane after a 1910 licence was granted to George Algernon lerring to show films. Memories of the hall are vivid – Gladys Brown wrote of her childhood eminiscences: 'The [picture] show was run by George Herring and his sons Stanley and Gordon nd, being a family affair, it was all very friendly and casual. As the time for a performance pproached, a crowd began to assemble outside the hall; there were no queues. Eventually one r both of the heavy wooden doors would be opened and there was quite a scramble to get nside. Halfway along was stationed the cashier, a Mr Wakefield, who pocketed the coins; he ad retired from the village police force and nobody would have thought of trying to slip in ithout paying when he was around'. Later she recalled: 'Often Mr Herring, to whip up nthusiasm, would stand on the steps of the 'Oasis' and call out the merits of the pictures being own. During the actual showing of the film, Gordon Herring would mount the steps near the age and read out the titles as they appeared and give a running commentary as the situations nfolded. There were frequent breakdowns and Gordon would get us to sing or give us a story...' *outh Yorkshire Times and Woodhouse Express* 4/01/58).

The Woodhouse Picture Palace built in 1914 at the Market Place *c*. 1924 which today is part of the shopping precinct. After the closure of the Central Hall the Picture Palace showed the latest features until December 28th 1957. The last manager was Mr Booth.

A view looking back to the Market Place by Smith's sweet shop *c*. 1967. The 'Wizard' beyond the butchers and Cross Daggers, which sold haberdashery, was demolished soon after the picture was taken; the houses on Tannery Street were removed in the late 1960s.

A very old picture of Market Place and Tannery Street *c.* 1890. Notice the barbers pole on the left, which premises were later occupied by John Truman.

The Market Place with a view of the Cross Daggers and The Wizard *c.* 1960; on the right is Malthouse Lane and the Zion chapel.

Market Place and Tannery Street *c.* 1963. Tannery Street got its name from the tanneries situated along it and was first called 'Tanyard' Street. Locals sometimes refer to Tannery Street as 'Back Street' and Chapel Street as 'Front Street' – a confusing state of affairs for those from outside the village ! All the buildings pictured here in Tannery Street were pulled down in the late 1960s and Tannery Close flats stand on the site.

Malthouse Lane and the Zion chapel. The row of shops in the distance and the buildings on the right have since been pulled down.

Hardcastle's Yard c. 1900. A yard was an enclosed piece of land containing workshops and homes and a larger house owned by the person with enough money to maintian all the properties: the yards would usually be named after these prominent individuals and hence Hardcastle's Yard. Many of the old yards around Sheffield were swept away during the 1960s and 1970s. This particular yard stood at the back of Smith's sweet shop and was demolished to make way for the shopping precinct.

Hardcastle's Yard c. 1950.

Hardcastle's Yard *c.* 1950. The date stone of 1656 above one of the cottages shows when the yard was constructed but during the attempts to demolish the yard workers found evidence of much earlier buildings. It is possible, but open to debate, that the date stone refers to when the cottages underwent stone cladding.

The defunct Co-op store in the precinct *c.* 1970. The date stone in the top picture is now in the wall behind the tree.

The old date stone forms part of the boundary wall at the shopping precinct.

A view of Cross Street taken from the Market Place in 1967.

Cross Street looking toward the St Paul's Methodist chapel; on the right is the Spar store and Jack Manning's green grocery shop.

Cross Street c. 1967. Melia's supermarket, which is now Dickinson's hardware store, is on the left of the street.

Looking down Cross Street in 1965; on the left is J.T. Dobson Ltd clothing shop; the houses in the background were on Malthouse Lane.

Looking down Cross Street in the 1930s. The shops in the centre of the photograph were later demolished and rebuilt in line with the Royal toward the end of the street; on the right is Manor House and James Hall's bakery shop (the bakehouse being to the rear of the premises).

Two views of Market Street in the 1960s. In the second picture Hardcastle's Yard, though ramshackle, is visible on the right, and just behind the War Memorial.

A view of the cross in the Market Place c. 1900 looking in the direction of Cross Street.

Jack Dyson sits in the stocks in the Market Place in 1929 when the two wooden beams were put back between the stone lintels. The last 'customers' to be placed in the stocks in 1820 were Bill Sykes and William Broad after being arrested by Constable Robert Hawksworth for being drunk and disorderly.

Bob Cavill at the Market Place in 1920. Bob broke his back in the mines and this special carriage was constructed by friends and relatives to move him about. During travels to football matches Bob was allowed to ride in the guard's carriage.

Three
Public Houses and Clubs

The Cross Daggers at the Market Place c. 1970. The date 1658 over the door with the letters NTG make the Cross Daggers by far the oldest dated building in the village, and from the few remaining records it appears that it was built by Thomas Godfrey Newbould, a Quaker and one of the biggest local landlords. Although little is known of the intervening history of the building, it seems that when built, the inn brewed its own beer in a building at the back, a building which was demolished in the 1930s. In 1758 Thomas Rawson's brewery in Pond Street was founded, and at an unknown date Rawsons became he owners of the public house. The inn was run by the Staniforth family for over 150 years; the last member of the family, Mary Redfearn, held the licence until 1958 when Fred Hobson took over. In 1965, and until its closure in the 1970s, the inn was run by James and Edna Meadows for Tetley's of Leeds. In all its history the beer at the Cross Daggers was always 'drawn from the wood', i.e. there were no pumps to put a froth on the beer, only a tap from the barrel.

As well as a noted public house, the Cross Daggers had been a collection point for letters before Woodhouse had a post office. In 1850, it was reported that a man named Zell used to walk from Sheffield via Attercliffe and Handsworth, arriving around noon with the village's letters.

The old Angel Inn on Chapel Street in 1920. The inn was situated opposite Mr Shepherd's shop (now Janine's) and was demolished in 1925 for road widening. Williamson Brothers' garage later occupied the site. It was shown on a plan of 1800 as being kept by a Mr T. Widdiwson and up to the year of 1862 it was called The Bull. The sport of bull baiting had taken place upon the village green but was outlawed in 1836 and this may have been the reason for a change in name.

Prospect House in 1908, the home of Mr and Mrs Charles Newton, was later to be converted into the Angel Inn. Ernest Dyson was the first landlord.

The Angel Inn in 1950 after the move to Prospect House.

A view in 1966 of the Angel. The inn now belongs to the Stone's brewery but it had previously been owned by Hope and Anchor, Truswell's and Tetley's.

John William Cook stands in the doorway of the Stag Inn *c.* 1900. Although the newest of the village's public houses before it was enlarged seventy years ago, the date 1721 could be seen over the doorway. It was a private house and the home of Samuel Atkin who owned a bakehouse and a windmill in Woodhouse. John Cook, landlord from 1885 to 1909, was also the bandmaster of the Woodhouse Prize Band. From 1964 to 1982 it was kept by George and Joyce Woodhouse and then by James McGuigan until 1991. The present incumbent is David Wales.

The Stag after extensions had been made at the side of the building c. 1909. The yard at the front of the pub was often the venue for market stalls and occasional visits by 'Cheap Jacks' who sold watches, clocks, jewellery, crockery and ornaments.

The George Inn c. 1905. The inn was originally built as a farmhouse by a Mr Birks in the early part of the nineteenth century. As the country was ruled by the Hanoverian Kings at this time it was probably named after one of the 'Georgian' monarchs. The earliest recorded landlord is John Staniforth in 1856 but at the time of this picture the tenure was held by Albert Bird. The building here still resembles a farmhouse with its five great sash windows and is almost unrecognisable when compared with the modern building shown on the next page.

The George Inn *c.* 1975. The landlords that followed Albert Bird were: John Wheatley, Stephen Waterhouse, Jaberz Cox, Ronald Morley, Percy Smith, Ronald Pugsley, Percy and Ada Bower, Michael Attwood. Since 1990 the landlord has been Paul Dawson.

Mr and Mrs Lomas, landlord and landlady, outside The Royal Hotel *c.* 1930. In 1822, a William Champion is listed as having a public house called the Bull's Head on the site of the present Royal Hotel. By 1851 it was kept by a Joseph Taylor and was known as The Coach and Horses ten years after it became The Royal Hotel with Thomas Garner the landlord. After Mr and Mrs Lomas gave up tenure the Hotel was renovated, extended and given the appearance it ha today.

The Junction Inn *c.* 1910 when it was kept by Robert Pashley. The large open shelter on the right has since been demolished. For thirty eight years the inn was kept by John Dale Hollis (1923-1961) and owned by Rawson's (later Tetley's).

The W.M. Central Club on Beighton Road *c.* 1968 was earlier called The Lambcroft.

East Woodhouse Distress Fund outside the Woodhouse Workingmen's Club and Institute c. 1921. Those identified so far are: Mrs Longbottom (seated, second left), Councillor Atkin (standing, far left), Miss K. Longbottom (standing, second from right). The Salvation Army officers are Mr and Mrs McArdle.

A gathering outside the Woodhouse Working Men's Club on Balmoral Road c. 1923. This club was to close before the Second World War and became a shop supplying gardeners and pet owners.

Four
Shops and Businesses

The Co-operative Society was started in Woodhouse in 1857 by Charles Mirfin who had been inspired by the founders of the movement, the Rochdale Pioneers. The first shop in the Market Place sold only four items – flour, sugar, tea, soap – all of which would have been essentials to Woodhouse family. Fired by the enthusiasm shown by Mr Mirfin, a group of Woodhouse miners banded together to open a small store on Chapel Street; it was formally registered in 1861 and opened until 11 p.m. The Society was run on an entirely voluntary basis until the turn of the century when it was taken over by Robert Walker. He served as President for nineteen years and brought the Society into the commercial world. The dividend rose throughout his presidency to a high of 2s 6d.

A view of Chapel Street c. 1965. The shop in the centre was Mr Fielding's (pet and garden) and was the Co-op store referred to on the previous page.

For many people living during the inter-war years the Co-operative was an imperative. Everyone had a membership number and looked forward to the dividend pay-out. Schools sometimes even gave classes in how and why the Society had been formed.

During the General Strike of 1926 the Woodhouse Co-operative baked 1, 729 loaves, free of charge, for distribution to workers families. At the back is the Co-op manager Mr Platts. Front: Reg Hempsall, Fred Walker, Charles Grundy.

Henry Wheeler's barber shop on Tannery Street in 1965. After the demolition of this building in the 1970s Mr Wheeler moved to premises on Chapel Street (the shop with the awning on page 58). The man walking his dog is thought to be Mr Percy Haynes.

Wheeler's barber shop had previously been Keyworth's butchers. On the right stands Jones and Faulkner's boot warehouse *c.* 1898.

Jones and Faulkner's boot warehouse on Tannery Street *c.* 1900. These premises later became Mr Orange's wallpaper shop. Mr Vivian Kendall is on the left.

Shepherd's drapery shop and millinery business on Chapel Street c. 1900.

A poster announcing a sale at Shepherd's in 1937. Today the shop is the site of Janine's children's clothing.

1937

SHEPHERD'S SALE

AT 16 CHAPEL STREET, WOODHOUSE,
COMMENCES
On FRIDAY, JANUARY 22nd, at 10 o'clock,
FOR NINE DAYS ONLY.

Special Offers.

LADIES.	FROM	GENTLEMEN.	FROM
◊Art Silk Hose	6½d.	Tunic Shirts, two Collars, Horrock's Print, all sizes	2/11½
Interlock Pyjamas, worth 5 11 ...	2 11½	◊Athletic Vests and Trunks	3½d.
◊Fleecy Lined Leatherette Coats	3 11	◊Wool Lined Nappa Gloves	3/11
"XOS" Fleecy Knickers ...	1/-	Ties	3½d.
◊Dressing Gowns	1/-	Handkerchiefs, woven border	3½d.
Wool Jumpers	1 6	◊Handkerchiefs, White Hemstitched 4 for 1/-	
◊Art Silk Nightdresses	1 6		
Vests	6½d.	Scarves	6½d.
O.S. Overalls	1/-	Winceyettte Pyjamas ...	3/11

CHILDREN.	FROM	GENERAL.	FROM
◊Fleecy Lined Leatherette Coat and Hat Sets, large sizes worth 6 11	3 11	◊48 in. Shadow Crettonne ...	9½d.
◊Jumpers, all sizes	9½d.	◊Large White Hemmed Towels, 24 in. x 46 in.	1 3
Wool Suits	1/-	Large Coloured Towels 6½d., 9½d. & 1/-	
T.O.T. Hose	3½d.		
Tennis Shirts, 2 to 6 ...	1/-	Lace Cheval Sets	6½d.
Silk Striped Knickers ...	6½d.	Pillow Slips, Guaranteed	
Flannelette Skirts	6½d.	Pure	6½d.

ALL WINTER GLOVES AND MILLINERY VERY MUCH REDUCED TO CLEAR

Mr Cutt's grocery shop on the corner of Chapel Street and Vicar Lane was situated next to Kendall's shoe shop *c.* 1910.

Popple Brothers shop in the Market Place *c.* 1920. These premises later became 'The Wizard'.

Prudential Assurance Company Limited office at the top of the Market Place (Coo Hill) *c.* 1950. This was demolished in the 1960s to make way for the shopping precinct. The source of the name 'Coo Hill' is uncertain but some locals insist it comes from the 'cooing' of the birds around the Market Place.

George Hawksworth's butchers on Coo Hill (Market Place) today stands empty. The premises have had a rapid turnover of owners including: cobblers, Julie's clothing, Yvette's children's wear, Sandra's clothing.

Glover and Company, family grocers and drapers, Market Street *c.* 1890.

A picture of the same building in the 1940s when it was owned by the Meadow Dairy Company Limited ('the firm that never sold a bad egg'). Left to right, the staff are: Alwyn Hazzard, Mr Smillye (manager), Ernest Percival, George Bygraves.

Cyril Crossland's newsagents shop on Market Street in 1960; it was eventually demolished to make way for the Job Centre.

Crossland's newsagents when the business was owned by Cyril's father c. 1920.

Looking up Hoyland Lane *c*. 1966. Crossland's newsagents is on the right; to the left was the pre-veg company, which earlier had been Edgar Keeton's butcher's shop before a move to Cross Street. Most of this area was demolished to make room for Stag Inn car park and the nearby Woodhouse Garden flats.

Mr James Starbuck's bakers at the top of Station Road *c*. 1900.

Hunsley's chip shop (previously owned by Mr Breckley), Sheffield Road c. 1960. The archway seen here led into Pashley's Cottages which is now the site of Tannery Lodge.

Frank Ledgard's grocery shop on the corner of Sheffield Road and Victoria Road c. 1920.

Joe Pearson stands outside his father's grocery shop on Sheffield Road *c.* 1930. The shop now belongs to Spar.

Five

Days of Learning

Woodhouse Grammar school on Station Road was built in 1909 and came under the old West Riding Education Authority. Today the building is used as a community centre.

In 1870 Forster's Education Act was passed instituting state funded and maintained elementary schools; this was designed to fill in the gaps in the existing voluntary system by the creation of a local authority and school board. By the late Victorian period consensus had finally concluded that the working classes were no longer the 'swinnish herd' but the future of a nation. The Reform Act of 1867 and the Forster Act were the start of a long (and painfully slow) period of necessary change. The realisation that the old order could no longer be sustained had become ingrained; change would take place through revolution or reform. As Robert Lowe's popular dictum of the day stated ('We must educate our future masters') the seeds for twentieth century success would have to be sown early. In 1889 the West Riding Authority built the Woodhouse Board school on Station Road under the auspecies of the Act with accommodation for 837 scholars (400 seniors and 437 juniors).

Endowed Church of England school was built in 1848 and situated on the corner of Chapel Street, Waterslacks Lane and Tannery Street. This picture from the 1960s shows the old school just before the road alterations necessitated their demolition.

Woodhouse West School on Sheffield Road *c.* 1930. The building, which today serves as a training centre, was built in 1900. The first headmaster, Mr Crowther, had been in charge at the Birley school in Normanton Springs, the Endowed school and later Station Road school.

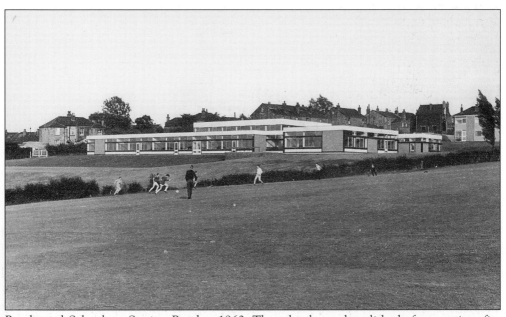

Brockwood School on Station Road *c.* 1960. The school was demolished after a serious fire gutted many of the classrooms; a replacement, the Brunswick Primary school, was built soon after. The name 'Brock' means badger and it is possible that the fields round had several badger sets.

A class from Woodhouse West in 1933. Back row, left to right: Peggy Hardy, Margaret Mellors, Irene Mellors, Joe Pearson, Frank Holdsworth, Harry Berresford, Arthur Turtle, Norman Coulson, Sylvia Mellors. Second row: -?-, Blanche Reilly, John Tempest, Eric Widdowson, Mary Mcallum, Pat Fleming, Jack Newbould, Rose Smith, Gerald Osborne, Peggy Scott, Frank Turner. Third row: Ada Jackson, Queenie Hardy, Eric Williamson, ? Sutton, Bernard Burchick, Elsie Shaw, Leslie Shaw, Charlie Pridmore, Clarence Walker, ? Watson. Front row: Jane Smith, Arnold Reilly, Violet Froggatt, Evelyn Williams, ? Grice, Bill Lax, Arthur Lowe, Willis Gregg.

Sally Clark's cottage c. 1900. The cottage, as we shall see later, served many purposes but in the middle of the last century it was a 'Dame school'.

A Birks Brothers coach on a trip to Matlock in 1922. The Birks were an old Woodhouse family – Birks Avenue is their testament today.

A Cutt's wagonette at the corner of Station Road and Brighton Road, Woodhouse in the 1930s.

A mobile 'soap' van at the bottom of Victoria Road *c.* 1935. With most of Woodhouse's population employed at the pit or on the railway a regular supply of soap must have been essential.

The Great Central Station at Woodhouse *c.* 1910. The line, which connects Sheffield and Worksop, was laid by the London North East Railway Company in 1849.

An eastward view of the Grand Central Station in 1910. The original station for this line was near Junction Lane but this 'grander' version was built in 1870.

The collision of engines at Woodhouse Junction on February 29th 1908. A mineral train leaving the East Junction was shunted from behind by an 'emigrant' special with 300 hundred passengers aboard travelling from Liverpool to Grimsby. The impact caused the death of mineral train guard and fatally wounded the fireman. Walter Howell, the driver of the mineral train was badly injured but the driver and fireman of the Liverpool train were unhurt despite their engine being almost overturned.

A locomotive passes Driver Street at Woodhouse Station in June 1963. This particular line has since been removed. The houses in the background are in Horsewood Road.

A view past the station and footbridge with Driver Street in the background *c.* 1960

Birley East Pit, Woodhouse *c.* 1923. It is difficult to imagine today where Woodhouse's main employer was situated; a point Alan Rowles makes in his excellent history of the colliery. 'If, like me, you were born and bred in the village, you will no doubt remember that prior to 1950, Woodhouse had just such a colliery on its doorstep. You will also almost certainly know that along with many of the old buildings which once graced the village, the pit in question, Birley East, has to all intents and purposes, vanished off the face of the Earth. Like your old house and street, like the chapels and cinema, like the surrounding farmland, the pit has vanished with such a finality that it may never have existed, except in the imagination. Although Woodhouse was never a 'pit village' in the true sense of the term it is certainly a fact that for many years Birley East was the district's principal employer, with, in its heyday well over 1,000 men on the payroll.' (Rowles, A. (1992). *Winding up – A History of Birley East Colliery*).

William Gainsford with his son standing next to a colliery engine, *Birley No.3.* c. 1900. Gainsford's family was one of the original shareholders in the Sheffield Coal Company; their expansion plans in 1887 included the sinking of a shaft at Fustian Wells between Woodhouse and Hackenthorpe near to Spa Lane. The last of the seams, Thorncliffe, was abandoned in 1948 and Birley East ceased production.

A Birley Coal Wagon *c.* 1925. Most of the wagons used by the Sheffield Coal Company were leased from such companies as the British Wagon Company and Lincoln Wagon and Engine Company. As Alan Rowles suggested in his history the Birley name was carried on all the wagons as 'a relatively cheap but effective method of advertising, and bought the company name to the attention of a great many prospective customers.'

Birley Engine No.3 *c.* 1910. This engine was one of six ordered from Peckett and Sons of Bristol; it arrived at Birley in 1903. Her short wheelbase made her ideal for the tight track curves around Birley West. After 1926 she was transferred to Beighton and then to Brookhouse, finally being scrapped during the war.

A group of pit ponies and workers outside the colliery offices *c.* 1910.

Seven

Around Market Street, Beever Hill Road and Shortcliffe Wood

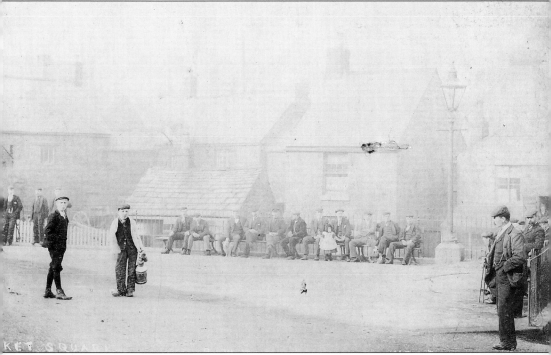

Market Street c. 1900. The roadside railings on the far side of the street were put up by the Handsworth and Woodhouse Urban District Council in 1898.

Orchard Terrace, which stood between Back Lane and Market Street, was demolished in the 1960s. The Stag Inn is at the far end of the street and the small cottage building in the centre was a regular practice site for the Woodhouse brass band.

Market Street *c.* 1970. The large building on the right was Keeton's the undertakers. This view would have been obscured until the removal of Farmyard cottages (see the next picture).

Shirtcliffe Dyke at Carr Lane *c.* 1900. Little has changed from this tranquil scene at the turn of the century. The black poplar tree on the left remains resolutely standing today.

Shirtcliffe Bank *c.* 1910.

In the Shirtcliffe Woods at the turn of the century.

Woodhouse maisonettes were built in the early 1960s as short term housing for the influx of a new population from the 'suburbs' of Attercliffe and Darnall but remained until only recently when they were replaced by a new estate.

Eight

Station Road and Beighton Road

The top of Station Road in 1903 with Market Street on the left. Every home and shop on this picture has since been demolished.

Children leave the Board school on Station Road in 1905. The buildings as far as the school have all since been demolished.

Station Road with the old Conservative Club on the distant right *c.* 1905.

The Conservative Club on Station Road *c*. 1930. Mr and Mrs Taylor, the stewards, lived in an adjacent house.

A view down Station Road in 1910 with a bread delivery van on the left; the area to the right is now the site of several houses.

An E. L. Scriven's picture of Station Road *c*. 1910. The wooden structure on the left is Edward's grocery shop. Most of this area remains unchanged although the wall and trees of Netherfield Hall (right) have been removed.

Netherfield Hall was built by George Ward in 1870 and demolished in the 1930s; the site is now open fields.

The end of Junction Lane *c.* 1950. The tracks to the left once went to Birley East colliery but have long since been dug up; the signal box that remains is the only reminder.

Beighton Road in 1914. The left side of this picture is virtually unchanged from that of a contemporary view; on the right stood the Central Club (now Balmoral nursing home) and the background shows a large telegraph pole indicating the presence of the nearby telephone exchange in Bridby Street run by Mrs Turner.

Beighton Road *c*. 1920. The houses here on the right were demolished during road widening. The area on the right today contains the Oldale estate which was named after a property owner from the 1800s Matthew Oldale.

Nine
Tannery Street and Skelton Lane

Tanyard workers at the corner of Birks Avenue and Tannery Street c. 1895. The stacks of oak bark stored in the background are an essential part of the tanning process.

A soup kitchen outside Keyworth House on Tannery Street in 1912.

A view from Keyworth's looking up Tannery Street. Part of the Tannery buildings are on the right.

Two contemporary views of Tannery Street before the demolition of the south side.

The top of Tannery Street and Skelton Lane *c.* 1910. The left side of this picture is now a modern housing estate; the library was later built on site to the right. The Coffee and Cocoa Rooms (page 61) are in the centre. The Wesleyan chapel and schoolroom is in the background

Woodhouse Library was opened by Alderman Harold W. Jackson, the Lord Mayor of Sheffield on May 20th 1931. The building was designed and constructed under the direction of the City Architect, Mr W.G. Davies, and built by the Direct Labour Department of the City Corporation. Messrs. T.B. and W. Cockayne, and Messrs. Thos. Wilkinson and Sons Ltd supplied the furniture of the junior and adult libraries respectively. The total cost of the project (excluding the site) was £4, 800 with a first year book provision of £1,100.

Tannery Street c. 1905. The house in the centre of this picture belonged to Mrs Jarvis but today it forms part of the car park for the new Co-op. Swann's shop is on the right with the gas lamp. Behind the wall was the City Council Public Works Yard.

The vestry office c. 1908 was built in 1838 and is the contemporary site for the offices of the Halifax Building Society.

At the side of the vestry was the Endowed school.

The caretakers cottage for the Endowed school was situated behind the vestry.

Sally Clark's cottage *c.* 1904. Sally Clark, who lived in this cottage during the 1800s, was believed to be a witch by many local people. Over the years, as well as being a home, Sally Clark's cottage had a number of different uses including a Dame school, a dance room and even a Cholera hospital. The last tenant to occupy the cottage was a Joseph Arnold, with one of his sons and a lodger called Mr Froggert. Around 1940 the cottage became unoccupied and then, sadly, was repeatedly vandalised. Shortly afterwards it was demolished to allow opencast mining to take place. Today, this area is still referred to by many local people as Sally Clark's, and the steep south facing slopes have become an important site for nature conservation. Its original name was Gaping Hill Cottage and it was the home of Joshua Sargeant, a miller who had a windmill to the right of the cottage. The windmill was in working order in 1795.

The top of Malthouse Lane in 1966.

Ten
Chapel Street, Vicar Lane and Cross Street

A view down Chapel Street from just outside the Co-op *c.* 1905. The Wesleyan chapel is pictured on the right.

Chapel Street *c.* 1965. The Dolphin pet store (left) has since been demolished.

A view of Vicar Lane in 1910 that remains unchanged today.

Cross Street with St Paul's Methodist chapel in the centre c. 1966. Kendall's shoe shop is on the left; the houses on the right are now shops. The house next to the yard entrance belonged to Miss Potter.

Miss Potter in her home on Cross Street.

An E.L. Scriven's picture of Cross Street. The postcard has been incorrectly titled Chapel Street.

Walter Hall, the GPO telegram boy, stands in full uniform next to a loaded buggy on Cross Street. This shop is currently empty.

Eleven

The West End

The old Police station on Waterslacks Lane later became an Adult Centre.

The old Co-op Hall on Tannery Street and Sheffield Road *c*. 1960. The grass area in the front of this picture was the 'pinfold' – a pen for animals that had managed to gain freedom from local fields and gardens. The animals were kept in the pen until the owner paid a specified fine.

PARK DRIVE CIGARETTES

Sheffield Road in 1960. The old Police station is in the centre; Callaby's shop is to the right.

Sheffield Road *c.* 1962 with the Vestry in the far background.

The stone cottages on Waterslacks Lane with Sheffield Road in the background *c.* 1965.

Sheffield Road c. 1965. The open area to the right is now the site for Skelton Grove flats; the old cottage belonged to a Mr James Greenwood.

Mary cottage, Sheffield Road. The cottage probably got its name from a provision in the 1775 will of a Mary Ward leaving the property to her son George. The smaller building became a sweet shop, among other uses, and was last used as a meeting place for journalists from the *Woodhouse Express*. Those pictured are, left to right: Mrs Guymer, Ben and Alice Dale (and their children Olive and Doris), Christine Good, Mrs Fielding.

Sheffield Road *c.* 1905. Stanley Widdowson stands with his dog amongst this group of locals; in the background is Woolfall's shop.

Twitchell cottages *c.* 1960 connected Sheffield Road with Bishop Hill but are today the site of a bungalow.

A view up Victoria Road *c.* 1970. Houses 6 and 7 (conspicuous by their white painted window frames) are the only houses which survived demolition on that side in the 1970s.

Two views of Victoria Road. All these buildings apart from two bay-windowed houses and an obscured fish and chip shop were pulled down in the clearances of the 1960s and 1970s.

The corner of Victoria Road and Sheffield Road *c.* 1970. Today the only remaining houses are Hygenic Villas on Sheffield Road (no's 129, 131, 133, 135).

Jack Davies, a local brush salesman, demonstrates his wares on Victoria Road *c.* 1930.

A '19' bus passes Woodhouse West End School on its route between Dinnington and Sheffield.

Looking down Sheffield Road in 1930. The buildings on the right-side of this picture remain but over the road a new housing estate was built in the 1970s.

Houses on Sheffield Road just before demolition in 1979. The only survivors are the nearest house and the half-shown house at the extreme left.

Normanton Springs *c.* 1966. The terraces at the bottom of the picture were demolished to make way for the Mosborough Parkway which heralded the start of the new townships.

Twelve
Woodhouse Mill

The iron bridge on Retford Road c. 1935. A walkway has since been added on the left of this picture.

Woodhouse Mill, Handsworth Rd.

A view taken from near the bridge looking down Retford Road (previously called Handsworth Road). Horsewood Road is on the right; the land on the left belonged to Coalbrook Farm.

A view looking from Furnace Lane along Retford Road in the direction of the Iron Bridge c. 1910.

Ada Baker stands outside her shop on Retford Road c. 1923.

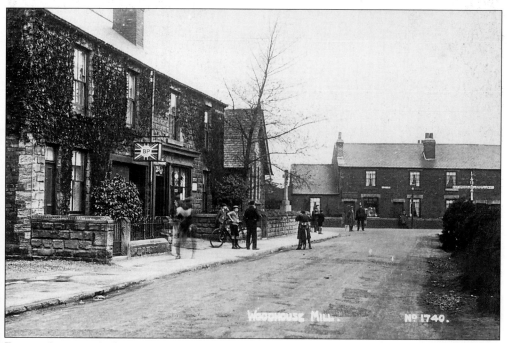

Furnace Lane c. 1925.

Coalbrook Crescent *c*. 1920. The Crescent was an island created by the division of the River Rother. The estate was built to house workers from the nearby Rotherwood iron works. Many locals knew the area as 'Canary Island' as the swampy land was ideal breeding ground for Canary Reed Grass. The estate was pulled down in the 1960s and is now the site of the sewage works and a petrol station.

The old mill (which became the shovel works) and weir on the River Rother *c*. 1930.

Thirteen
Woodhouse People and the Band

The reception for the wedding of Emma Birks to Albert Davidson outside Holly House June 22nd 1896.

A group outside Woodhouse District Nurses Home on Stradbrooke Road April 1931. Left to right: Harry Staniforth, William Widdowson, William Morley (secretary of Beighton colliery N.U.M.), Rev L.R. Healey, Herbert Smith (President of Barnsley N.U.M.), Councillor William Furniss, Alderman Sir Harold Jackson (Lord Mayor of Sheffield), Mrs W. Morley, Richard Brindley, Nurse Chapman, Clem Wells, -?-.

Woodhouse Prize band of 1888. Back row, left to right: J. W. Cook (bandmaster), T. Cook, H. Cook, A. Pye. Middle row: William Cook (senior), E. Cook, H. Cook, T. Parramore, J. Cook, E. Burgess. Front row: E. Spruce, W. Clayton, B. Cook, J. Wright, E. Atkinson, J. Grundy, A. Morton.

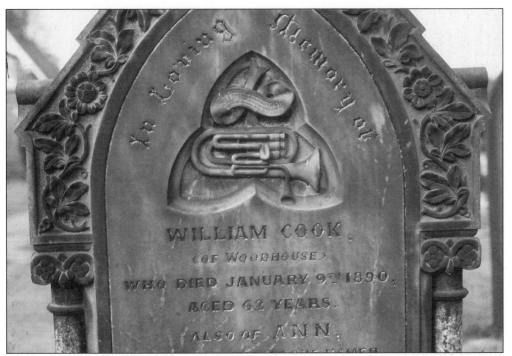

The headstone of William Cook of the Woodhouse Prize band. Over 5,000 people attended the funeral procession from the Stag Inn to the cemetery.

Woodhouse Prize band in the 1920s on the church croft.

A centenary photograph of the Woodhouse Prize band in 1953. Members of the band in this year were: A. Young, A. Jackson, P. Jackson, W. Ruff, C. Cartwright, G. Cook, G. Truman, R. Truman, R. Burgin, R. Hancock, B. Hardy, J. Grice, A. Oldroyd, A. Cartwright, A. Clarke, B. Hancock, L.W. Cartwright, W. Burgin, S. Kay, W. Collins, T. Richards, J.H. Young, J.J. Hancock, W. Turner, C. Young, W.E. Herbert, H. Cook, H.R. Brown.

The band in the 1980s included Mr G. Cook, Mr K. Varley, Mr F. Metcalfe, Mr N. Cawkwell, Mr D. Drinkwater.